Marlborough & Other Poems by Charles Sorley

Charles Hamilton Sorley was born on May 19th, 1895 in Aberdeen. His family moved to Cambridge when Sorley was five and his education later continued at Marlborough College (1908-13) where he was an excellent debater.

From here he won a scholarship to Oxford but decided to spend a year in Germany beforehand. It was a fateful decision. War clouds had gathered over Europe and when war was declared Sorley was interned, for one night, and then instructed to leave Germany.

Sorley returned to England and immediately signed up to serve as a 2nd Lieutenant with the Suffolk Regiment. He arrived in France in May, 1915 and, by the same August, had been promoted to Captain.

On October 13th 1915, at the Battle of Loos, Charles Hamilton Sorley was killed by a sniper's bullet to the head.

From far away there comes a Voice,
Singing its song across the sea—

I0158434

A song to make man's heart rejoice—
Of Marlborough and the Odyssey.

A voice that sings of Now and Then,
Of minstrel joys and tiny towns.

Of flowering thyme and fighting men.
Of Sparta's sands and Marlborough's Downs.

God grant, dear Voice, one day again
We see those Downs in April weather.

And snuff the breeze, and smell the rain.
And stand in C House Porch together!

Index of Contents
Preface
Marlborough
Barbury Camp
What you will
Rooks
Rooks (II)
Stones
East Kennet Church at Evening
Autumn Dawn
Return
Richard Jefferies
J. B.

The Other Wise Man
The Song of the Ungirt Runners
German Rain
Whom Therefore We Ignorantly Worship
To Poets
A Hundred Thousand Million Mites We Go
Deus loquitur
Two Songs from Ibsen's Dramatic Poems
"If I Have Suffered Pain"
To Germany
All the Hills and Vales Along
Le Revenant
Lost
Expectans Expectavi
TWO SONNETS
I - Saints Have Adored the Lofty Soul of You
II - Such, Such is Death: No triumph: No defeat
A Sonnet - When you see millions of the Mouthless Dead
There is Such Change in All Those Fields
I Have Not Brought My Odyssey
In Memoriam S.C.W., V.C
Behind the Lines
EARLIER POEMS
A Call to Action
Rain
A Tale of Two Careers
Peace
The River
The Seekers

PREFACE

What was said concerning the author in the preface to the first edition may be repeated here. He was born at Old Aberdeen on 19 May 1895. From 1900 onwards his home was in Cambridge. He was at Marlborough College from September 1908 till December 1913, when he was elected to a scholarship at University College, Oxford. After leaving school he spent a little more than six months in Germany, returning home on the outbreak of war. He was gazetted Second Lieutenant in the Seventh (Service) Battalion of the Suffolk Regiment in August 1914, Lieutenant in November, and Captain in the following August. His battalion was sent to France on 30 May. He was killed in action near Hulluch on 13 October 1915. "Being made perfect in a little while, he fulfilled long years."

Many readers have asked for further information about the author or contributions from his pen. I am not able to give all that is asked for; but in this edition I have done what I can to meet the wishes of my correspondents by appending to the poems a certain number of illustrations in prose. With the exception of a few sentences from an early essay, these prose passages are all taken from his letters to his family and friends. They have been selected as illustrating some idea or subject mentioned in the poems and prominent in his own mind.

But the relevancy is not always very close; the moods of the moment are sometimes expressed rather than matured judgments; and it has to be remembered that what was written was not intended for other eyes than those of the person to whom it was addressed.

With the poems it is different; and, had he lived, he would probably himself have published a selection of them with such revision as he deemed advisable. But when a suggestion about printing was made to him, soon after he had entered upon his life in the trenches of Flanders, he put the proposal aside as premature, adding "Besides, this is no time for olive yards and vineyards, more especially of the small-holdings type. For three years or the duration of the war, let be." His warfare is now accomplished, and his relatives have felt themselves free to publish.

The original order of the poems is retained in this edition. The first place is assigned to the title-poem; some early poems are printed at the end; the other contents are arranged in the order of their composition, as nearly as that order could be ascertained. When the date given includes the day of the month, it has been taken from the author's manuscript; some of the other dates are approximate. Of the undated poems, XIII to XVI were received from him in October 1914, XVII to XXIV in April 1915, xxvii was found in his kit sent back from France, and XXVIII (which appeared for the first time in the second edition) was sent to a friend towards the end of July 1915. A single piece of imaginative prose has been included amongst the poems.

Some further information regarding them has been obtained recently, XVI was written when he was at the Officers' Training Camp at Churn early in September 1914, and XVII a few days later, xv had its origin in his journey from Churn to join his regiment at Shorn cliff e on 18 September. The first draft of it was sent to a friend soon afterwards with the words: "enclosed the poem which eventually came out of the first day of term at Paddington. Not much trace of the origin left; but I think it should get a prize for being the first poem written since August 4th that isn't patriotic." This draft differs slightly from the final form of the poem, and instead of the present title ("Whom therefore we ignorantly worship"), it is preceded by the verse "And these all, having obtained a good report through faith, received not the promise." The poem called "Lost" (XXIV) was sent to the same friend in December 1914. "I have tried for long," he wrote, "to express in words the impression that the land north of Marlborough must leave"; and he added, "Simplicity, paucity of words, monotony almost, and mystery are necessary. I think I have got it at last." The signpost, which figures here as well as elsewhere in the poems, stands at "the junction of the grass tracks on the Aldbourne down—to Ogbourne, Marlborough, Mildenhall, and Aldbourne. It stands up quite alone."

Three of the poems at least—II, VIII, and XII—were written entirely in the open air. Concerning one of these he said, "'Autumn Dawn' has too much copy from Meredith in it, but I value it as being (with 'Return') a memento of my walk to Marlborough last September [1913]." Sending his "occasional budget" in April 1915 he said, "You will notice that most of what I have written is as hurried and angular as the handwriting: written out at different times and dirty with my pocket: but I have had no time for the final touch nor seem likely to have for some time, and so send them as they are. Nor have I had time to think out (as I usually do) a rigorous selection as fit for other eyes. So these are my explanations of the fall in quality. I like 'Le Revenant' best, being very interested in the previous and future experience of the character concerned: but it sadly needs the file."

The letter in verse, fragments of which are given on pages 73-78, was sent anonymously to an older friend whose connexion with Marlborough is commemorated in the poem entitled "J. B." J. B. discovered the authorship of the epistle by sending the envelope to a Marlborough master, and replied in the words which, by his permission, are printed on the opposite page.

W. R. S.

21 September 1916.

MARLBOROUGH

I

Crouched where the open upland billows down
Into the valley where the river flows.
She is as any other country town,
That little lives or marks or hears or knows.

And she can teach but little. She has not
The wonder and the surging and the roar
Of striving cities. Only things forgot
That once were beautiful, but now no more,

Has she to give us. Yet to one or two
She first brought knowledge, and it was for her
To open first our eyes, until we knew
How great, immeasurably great, we were.

I, who have walked along her downs in dreams,
And known her tenderness, and felt her might.
And sometimes by her meadows and her streams
Have drunk deep-storied secrets of delight,

Have had my moments there, when I have been
Unwittingly aware of something more,
Some beautiful aspect, that I had seen
With mute unspeculative eyes before;

Have had my times, when, though the earth did wear
Her self-same trees and grasses, I could see
The revelation that is always there,
But somehow is not always clear to me.

II

So, long ago, one halted on his way
And sent his company and cattle on;
His caravans trooped darkling far away
Into the night, and he was left alone.

And he was left alone. And, lo, a man
There wrestled with him till the break of day.
The brook was silent and the night was wan.
And when the dawn was come, he passed away.

The sinew of the hollow of his thigh
Was shrunken, as he wrestled there alone.
The brook was silent, but the dawn was nigh.
The stranger named him Israel and was gone.

And the sun rose on Jacob; and he knew
That he was no more Jacob, but had grown
A more immortal vaster spirit, who
Had seen God face to face, and still lived on.

The plain that seemed to stretch away to God,
The brook that saw and heard and knew no fear,
Were now the self-same soul as he who stood
And waited for his brother to draw near.

For God had wrestled with him, and was gone.
He looked around, and only God remained.
The dawn, the desert, he and God were one.
—And Esau came to meet him, travel-stained.

III

So, there, when sunset made the downs look new
And earth gave up her colours to the sky.
And far away the little city grew
Half into sight, new-visioned was my eye.

I, who have lived, and trod her lovely earth.
Raced with her winds and listened to her birds,
Have cared but little for their worldly worth
Nor sought to put my passion into words.

But now it's different; and I have no rest
Because my hand must search, dissect and spell
The beauty that is better not expressed.
The thing that all can feel, but none can tell.

1st March 1914

BARBURY CAMP

We burrowed night and day with tools of lead.
Heaped the bank up and cast it in a ring
And hurled the earth above. And Caesar said,
"Why, it is excellent. I like the thing."
We, who are dead.
Made it, and wrought, and Caesar liked the thing.

And here we strove, and here we felt each vein
Ice-bound, each limb fast-frozen, all night long.
And here we held communion with the rain
That lashed us into manhood with its thong,
Cleansing through pain.
And the wind visited us and made us strong.

Up from around us, numbers without name.
Strong men and naked, vast, on either hand
Pressing us in, they came. And the wind came
And bitter rain, turning grey all the land.
That was our game,
To fight with men and storms, and it was grand.

For many days we fought them, and our sweat
Watered the grass, making it spring up green.
Blooming for us. And, if the wind was wet.
Our blood wetted the wind, making it keen
With the hatred
And wrath and courage that our blood had been.

So, fighting men and winds and tempests, hot
With joy and hate and battle-lust, we fell
Where we fought. And God said, "Killed at last then?
What?
Ye that are too strong for heaven, too clean for hell,
(God said) stir not.
This be your heaven, or, if ye will, your hell."

So again we fight and wrestle, and again
Hurl the earth up and cast it in a ring.
But when the wind comes up, driving the rain
(Each rain-drop a fiery steed), and the mists rolling
Up from the plain,
This wild procession, this impetuous thing,

Hold us amazed. We mount the wind-cars, then
Whip up the steeds and drive through all the world,
Searching to find somewhere some brethren.
Sons of the winds and waters of the world.
We, who were men.
Have sought and found no men in all this world.

Wind, that has blown here always ceaselessly,
Bringing, if any man can understand.
Might to the mighty, freedom to the free;
Wind, that has caught us, cleansed us, made us grand.
Wind that is we
(We that were men)—make men in all this land.

That so may live and wrestle and hate that when
They fall at last exultant, as we fell,
And come to God, God may say, "Do you come then
Mildly enquiring, is it heaven or hell?
Why! Ye were men!
Back to your winds and rains. Be these your heaven and hell!"

24th March 1913

WHAT YOU WILL

O come and see, it's such a sight,
So many boys all doing right:
To see them underneath the yoke.
Blindfolded by the elder folk,
Move at a most impressive rate
Along the way that is called straight.
O, it is comforting to know
They're in the way they ought to go.
But don't you think it's far more gay
To see them slowly leave the way
And limp and loose themselves and fall?
O, that's the nicest thing of all.

I love to see this sight, for then
I know they are becoming men.
And they are tiring of the shrine
Where things are really not divine.

I do not know if it seems brave
The youthful spirit to enslave,
And hedge about, lest it should grow.
I don't know if it's better so
In the long end. I only know
That when I have a son of mine,
He shan't be made to droop and pine,
Bound down and forced by rule and rod
To serve a God who is no God.
But I'll put custom on the shelf
And make him find his God himself.

Perhaps he'll find him in a tree,
Some hollow trunk, where you can see.
Perhaps the daisies in the sod
Will open out and show him God.
Or will he meet him in the roar
Of breakers as they beat the shore?
Or in the spiky stars that shine?
Or in the rain (where I found mine)?

Or in the city's giant moan?
          —A God who will be all his own.
          To whom he can address a prayer
          And love him, for he is so fair,
          And see with eyes that are not dim
          And build a temple meet for him.

June 1913

ROOKS

There, where the rusty iron lies,
The rooks are cawing all the day.
Perhaps no man, until he dies.
Will understand them, what they say.

The evening makes the sky like clay.
The slow wind waits for night to rise.
The world is half-content. But they

Still trouble all the trees with cries,
That know, and cannot put away.
The yearning to the soul that flies
From day to night, from night to day.

21st June 1913

ROOKS (II)

There is such cry in all these birds,
More than can ever be express'd;
If I should put it into words,
You would agree it were not best
To wake such wonder from its rest.

But since to-night the world is still
And only they and I astir,
We are united, will to will.
By bondage tighter, tenderer
Than any lovers ever were.

And if, of too much labouring,
All that I see around should die
(There is such sleep in each green thing,
Such weariness in all the sky),
We would live on, these birds and I.

Yet how? since everything must pass
At evening with the sinking sun.
And Christ is gone, and Barabbas,
Judas and Jesus, gone, clean gone,
Then how shall I live on?

Yet surely, Judas must have heard
Amidst his torments the long cry
Of some lone Israelitish bird.
And on it, ere he went to die.
Thrown all his spirit's agony.

And that immortal cry which welled
For Judas, ever afterwards
Passion on passion still has swelled
And sweetened, till to-night these birds
Will take my words, will take my words,

And wrapping them in music meet
Will sing their spirit through the sky,
Strange and unsatisfied and sweet—
That, when stock-dead am I, am I,
O, these will never die!

July 1913

STONES

This field is almost white with stones
That cumber all its thirsty crust.
And underneath, I know, are bones.
And all around is death and dust.

And if you love a livelier hue—
O, if you love the youth of year.
When all is clean and green and new,
Depart. There is no summer here.

Albeit, to me there lingers yet
In this forbidding stony dress
The impotent and dim regret
For some forgotten restlessness.

Dumb, imperceptibly astir,
These relics of an ancient race,
These men, in whom the dead bones were,
Still fortifying their resting-place.

Their field of life was white with stones;

Good fruit to earth they never brought.
O, in these bleached and buried bones
Was neither love nor faith nor thought.

But like the wind in this bleak place.
Bitter and bleak and sharp they grew.
And bitterly they ran their race,
A brutal, bad. unkindly crew:

Souls like the dry earth, hearts like stone.
Brains like that barren bramble-tree:
Stern, sterile, senseless, mute, unknown—
But bold, O, bolder far than we!

14th July 1913

EAST KENNET CHURCH AT EVENING

I stood amongst the corn, and watched
The evening coming down.
The rising vale was like a queen,
And the dim church her crown.

Crown-like it stood against the hills.
Its form was passing fair.
I almost saw the tribes go up
To offer incense there.

And far below the long vale stretched.
As a sleeper she did seem
That after some brief restlessness
Has now begun to dream.

(All day the wakefulness of men,
Their lives and labours brief.
Have broken her long troubled sleep.
Now, evening brings relief.)

There was no motion there, nor sound.
She did not seem to rise.
Yet was she wrapping herself in
Her grey of night-disguise.

For now no church nor tree nor fold
Was visible to me:
Only that fading into one
Which God must sometimes see.

No coloured glory streaked the sky

To mark the sinking sun.
There was no redness in the west
To tell that day was done.

Only, the greyness of the eve
Grew fuller than before.
And, in its fulness, it made one
Of what had once been more.

There was much beauty in that sight
That man must not long see.
God dropped the kindly veil of night
Between its end and me.

24th July 1913

AUTUMN DAWN

And this is morning. Would you think
That this was the morning, when the land
Is full of heavy eyes that blink
Half-opened, and the tall trees stand
Too tired to shake away the drops
Of passing night that cling around
Their branches and weigh down their tops:
And the grey sky leans on the ground?
The thrush sings once or twice, but stops
Affrighted by the silent sound.
The sheep, scarce moving, munches, moans.
The slow herd mumbles, thick with phlegm.
The grey road-mender, hacking stones.
Is now become as one of them.

Old mother Earth has rubbed her eyes
And stayed, so senseless, lying down.
Old mother is too tired to rise
And lay aside her grey nightgown.
And come with singing and with strength
In loud exuberance of day.
Swift-darting. She is tired at length,
Done up, past bearing, you would say.

She'll come no more in lust of strife.
In hedges' leap, and wild birds' cries,
In winds that cut you like a knife,
In days of laughter and swift skies.
That palpably pulsate with life.
With life that kills, with life that dies.
But in a morning such as this

Is neither life nor death to see,
Only that state which some call bliss,
Grey hopeless immortality

Earth is at length bedrid. She is
Supinest of the things that be:
And stilly, heavy with long years,
Brings forth such days in dumb regret.
Immortal days, that rise in tears.
And cannot, though they strive to, set.

The mists do move. The wind takes breath.
The sun appeareth over there.
And with red fingers hasteneth
From Earth's grey bed the clothes to tear.
And strike the heavy mist's dank tent.
And Earth uprises with a sigh.
She is astir. She is not spent.
And yet she lives and yet can die.
The grey road-mender from the ditch
Looks up. He has not looked before.
The stunted tree sways like the witch
It was: 'tis living witch once more.

The winds are washen. In the deep
Dew of the morn they've washed. The skies
Are changing dress. The clumsy sheep
Bound, and earth's many bosoms rise,
And earth's green tresses spring and leap
About her brow. The earth has eyes,
The earth has voice, the earth has breath,
As o'er the land and through the air.
With winged sandals. Life and Death
Speed hand in hand—that winsome pair!

16th September 1913

RETURN

Still stand the downs so wise and wide?
Still shake the trees their tresses grey?
I thought their beauty might have died
Since I had been away.

I might have known the things I love,
The winds, the flocking birds' full cry.
The trees that toss, the downs that move,
Were longer things than I.

Lo, earth that bows before the wind,
With wild green children overgrown.
And all her bosoms, many-whinned.
Receive me as their own.

The birds are hushed and fled: the cows
Have ceased at last to make long moan.
They only think to browse and browse
Until the night is grown.

The wind is stiller than it was,
And dumbness holds the closing day.
The earth says not a word, because
It has no word to say.

The dear soft grasses under foot
Are silent to the listening ear.
Yet beauty never can be mute.
And some will always hear.

18th September 1913

RICHARD JEFFERIES

(Liddington Castle)

I see the vision of the Vale
Rise teeming to the rampart Down,
The fields and, far below, the pale
Red-roofedness of Swindon town.

But though I see all things remote,
I cannot see them with the eyes
With which ere now the man from Coate
Looked down and wondered and was wise.

He knew the healing balm of night,
The strong and sweeping joy of day,
The sensible and dear delight
Of life, the pity of decay.

And many wondrous words he wrote.
And something good to man he showed.
About the entering in of Coate,
There, on the dusty Swindon road.

19th September 1913

There's still a horse on Granham hill,
And still the Kennet moves, and still
Four Miler sways and is not still.
But where is her interpreter?

The downs are blown into dismay,
The stunted trees seem all astray,
Looking for someone clad in grey
And carrying a golf-club thing;

Who, them when he had lived among,
Gave them what they desired, a tongue.
Their words he gave them to be sung
Perhaps were few, but they were true.

The trees, the downs, on either hand,
Still stand, as he said they would stand.
But look, the rain in all the land
Makes all things dim with tears of him.

And recently the Kennet croons.
And winds are playing widowed tunes.
He has not left our "toun o' touns,"
But taken it away with him!

October, 1913

THE OTHER WISE MAN

SCENE: A valley with a wood on one side and a road running up to a distant hill: as it might be, the valley to the east of West Woods, that runs up to Oare Hill, only much larger.

TIME: Autumn.

Four Wise Men are marching hillward along the road.

One Wise Man
I wonder where the valley ends?
On, comrades, on.

Another Wise Man
The rain-red road,
Still shining sinuously, bends
Leagues upwards.

A Third Wise Man

To the hill, O friends,
To seek the star that once has glowed
Before us; turning not to right
Nor left, nor backward once looking.
Till we have clomb—and with the night
We see the King.

All the Wise Men
The King! The King!

The Third Wise Man
Long is the road but—

A Fourth Wise Man
Brother, see,
There, to the left, a very aisle
Composed of every sort of tree—

The First Wise Man
Still onward—

The Fourth Wise Man
Oak and beech and birch,
Like a church, but homelier than church.
The black trunks for its walls of tile;
Its roof, old leaves; its floor, beech nuts;
The squirrels its congregation—

The Second Wise Man
Tuts!
For still we journey—

The Fourth Wise Man
But the sun weaves
A water-web across the grass.
Binding their tops. You must not pass
The water cobweb.

The Third Wise Man
Hush! I say.
Onward and upward till the day—

The Fourth Wise Man
Brother, that tree has crimson leaves.
You'll never see its like again.
Don't miss it. Look, it's bright with rain—

The First Wise Man
O prating tongue. On, on.

The Fourth Wise Man

And there
A toad-stool, nay, a goblin stool.
No toad sat on a thing so fair.

Wait, while I pluck—and there's—and here's
A whole ring... what?... berries?

[*The* **Fourth Wise Man** *drops behind, botanizing.*

The Wisest of the remaining Three Wise Men
O fool!
Fool, fallen in this vale of tears
His hand had touched the plough: his eyes
Looked back: no more with us, his peers.
He'll climb the hill and front the skies
And see the Star, the King, the Prize.
But we, the seekers, we who see
Beyond the mists of transiency—
Our feet down in the valley still
Are set, our eyes are on the hill.
Last night the star of God has shone,
And so we journey, up and on,
With courage clad, with swiftness shod,
All thoughts of earth behind us cast,
Until we see the lights of God,
—And what will be the crown at last?

All Three Wise Men
On, on.

[*They pass on: it is already evening when the* **Other Wise Man** *limps along the road, still botanizing.*

The Other Wise Man
A vale of tears, they said!
A valley made of woes and fears,
To be passed by with muffled head
Quickly. I have not seen the tears,
Unless they take the rain for tears.
And certainly the place is wet.
Rain laden leaves are ever licking
Your cheeks and hands...! can't get on.
There's a toad-stool that wants picking.
There, just there, a little up,
What strange things to look upon
With pink hood and orange cup!

And there are acorns, yellow—green...
They said the King was at the end.
They must have been Wrong.
For here, here, I intend
To search for him, for surely here

Are all the wares of the old year.
And all the beauty and bright prize,
And all God's colours meetly showed.
Green for the grass, blue for the skies.
Red for the rain upon the road;
And anything you like for trees,
But chiefly yellow brown and gold.
Because the year is growing old
And loves to paint her children these.
I tried to follow... but, what do you think?
The mushrooms here are pink!
And there's old clover with black polls
Black-headed clover, black as coals.
And toad-stools, sleek as ink!
And there are such heaps of little turns
Off the road, wet with old rain:
Each little vegetable lane
Of moss and old decaying ferns,
Beautiful in decay,
Snatching a beauty from whatever may
Be their lot, dark-red and luscious: till there pass'd
Over the many-coloured earth a grey Film.
It was evening coming down at last.
And all things hid their faces, covering up
Their peak or hood or bonnet or bright cup
In greyness, and the beauty faded fast,
With all the many-coloured coat of day.
Then I looked up, and lo! the sunset sky
Had taken the beauty from the autumn earth.
Such colour, O such colour, could not die.
The trees stood black against such revelry
Of lemon-gold and purple and crimson dye.
And even as the trees, so I
Stood still and worshipped, though by evening's birth
I should have capped the hills and seen the King.
The King? The King?
I must be miles away from my journey's end;
The others must be now nearing
The summit, glad. By now they wend
Their way far, far, ahead, no doubt.
I wonder if they've reached the end.
If they have, I have not heard them shout.

1st December 1913

THE SONG OF THE UNGIRT RUNNERS

We swing ungirded hips,
And lightened are our eyes,

The rain is on our lips,
We do not run for prize.
We know not whom we trust
Nor whitherward we fare,
But we run because we must
Through the great wide air.

The waters of the seas
Are troubled as by storm.
The tempest strips the trees
And does not leave them warm.
Does the tearing tempest pause?
Do the tree-tops ask it why?
So we run without a cause
'Neath the big bare sky.

The rain is on our lips,
We do not run for prize.
But the storm the water whips
And the wave howls to the skies.
The winds arise and strike it
And scatter it like sand,
And we run because we like it
Through the broad bright land.

GERMAN RAIN

The heat came down and sapped away my powers.
The laden heat came down and drowned my brain,
Till through the weight of overcoming hours
I felt the rain.

Then suddenly I saw what more to see
I never thought: old things renewed, retrieved.
The rain that fell in England fell on me.
And I believed.

WHOM THEREFORE WE IGNORANTLY WORSHIP

These things are silent. Though it may be told
Of luminous deeds that lighten land and sea,
Strong sounding actions with broad minstrelsy
Of praise, strange hazards and adventures bold,
We hold to the old things that grow not old:
Blind, patient, hungry, hopeless (without fee
Of all our hunger and unhope are we).
To the first ultimate instinct, to God we hold.

They flicker, glitter, flicker. But we bide.
We, the blind weavers of an intense fate.
Asking but this—that we may be denied:
Desiring only desire insatiate,
Unheard, unnamed, unnoticed, crucified
To our unutterable faith, we wait.

TO POETS

We are the homeless, even as you,
Who hope and never can begin.
Our hearts are wounded through and through
Like yours, but our hearts bleed within.
We too make music, but our tones
'Scape not the barrier of our bones.

We have no comeliness like you.
We toil, unlovely, and we spin.
We start, return: we wind, undo:
We hope, we err, we strive, we sin,
We love: your love's not greater, but
The lips of our love's might stay shut.

We have the evil spirits too
That shake our soul with battle-din.
But we have an eviller spirit than you,
We have a dumb spirit within:
The exceeding bitter agony
But not the exceeding bitter cry.

A HUNDRED THOUSAND MILLION MITES WE GO

A hundred thousand million mites we go
Wheeling and tacking o'er the eternal plain,
Some black with death—and some are white with woe.
Who sent us forth? Who takes us home again?

And there is sound of hymns of praise—to whom?
And curses—on whom curses?—snap the air.
And there is hope goes hand in hand with gloom,
And blood and indignation and despair.

And there is murmuring of the multitude
And blindness and great blindness, until some
Step forth and challenge blind Vicissitude
Who tramples on them: so that fewer come.

And nations, ankle-deep in love or hate,
Throw darts or kisses all the unwitting hour
Beside the ominous unseen tide of fate;
And there is emptiness and drink and power.

And some are mounted on swift steeds of thought
And some drag sluggish feet of stable toil.
Yet all, as though they furiously sought,
Twist turn and tussle, close and cling and coil.

A hundred thousand million mites we sway
Writhing and tossing on the eternal plain.
Some black with death—but most are bright with Day!
Who sent us forth? Who brings us home again?

DEUS LOQUITUR

That's what I am: a thing of no desire,
With no path to discover and no plea
To offer up, so be my altar fire
May burn before the hearth continuously,
To be For wayward men a steadfast light to see.

They know me in the morning of their days,
But ere noontide forsake me, to discern
New lore and hear new riddles. But moonrays
Bring them back footsore, humble, bent, a-bum
To turn
And warm them by my fire which they did spurn.

They flock together like tired birds. "We sought
Full many stars in many skies to see.
But ever knowledge disappointment brought.
Thy light alone, Lord, burneth steadfastly."
Ah me!
Then it is I who fain would wayward be.

TWO SONGS FROM IBSEN'S DRAMATIC POEMS

I

BRAND

Thou trod'st the shifting sand path where man's race is.
The print of thy soft sandals is still clear.
I too have trodden it those prints a-near,

But the sea washes out my tired foot-traces.
And all that thou hast healed and holpen here
I yearned to heal and help and wipe the tear
Away. But still I trod unpeopled spaces.
I had no twelve to follow my pure paces.
For I had thy misgivings and thy fear,
Thy crown of scorn, thy suffering's sharp spear,
Thy hopes, thy longings—only not thy dear
Love (for my crying love would no man hear),
Thy will to love, but not thy love's sweet graces.
That deep firm foothold which no sea erases.
I think that thou wast I in bygone places
In an intense eliminated year.
Now born again in days that are more drear
I wander unfulfilled: and see strange faces.

II

PEER GYNT

When he was young and beautiful and bold
We hated him, for he was very strong.
But when he came back home again, quite old,
And wounded too, we could not hate him long.

For kingliness and conquest pranced he forth
Like some high-stepping charger bright with foam.
And south he strode and east and west and north
With need of crowns and never need of home.

Enraged we heard high tidings of his strength
And cursed his long forgetfulness. We swore
That should he come back home some eve at length.
We would deny him, we would bar the door!

And then he came. The sound of those tired feet!
And all our home and all our hearts are his,
Where bitterness, grown weary, turns to sweet.
And envy, purged by longing, pity is.

And pillows rest beneath the withering cheek,
And hands are laid the battered brows above,
And he whom we had hated, waxen weak.
First in his weakness learns a little love.

If I have suffered pain
It is because I would.
I willed it. 'Tis no good
To murmur or complain.
I have not served the law
That keeps the earth so fair
And gives her clothes to wear,
Raiment of joy and awe.

For all that bow to bless
That law shall sure abide.
But man shall not abide,
And hence his gloriousness.
Lo, evening earth doth lie
All-beauteous and all peace.
Man only does not cease
From striving and from cry.

Sun sets in peace: and soon
The moon will shower her peace.
O law-abiding moon,
You hold your peace in fee!
Man, leastways, will not be
Down-bounden to these laws.
Man's spirit sees no cause
To serve such laws as these.

There yet are many seas
For man to wander in.
He yet must find out sin,
If aught of pleasance there
Remain for him to store,
His rovings to increase,
In quest of many a shore
Forbidden still to fare.

Peace sleeps the earth upon,
And sweet peace on the hill.
The waves that whimper still
At their long law-serving
(O flowing sad complaint!)
Come on and are back drawn.
Man only owns no king,
Man only is not faint.

You see, the earth is bound.
You see, the man is free.
For glorious liberty
He suffers and would die.
Grudge not then suffering
Or chastisemental cry.

O let his pain abound.
Earth's truant and earth's king!

TO GERMANY

You are blind like us. Your hurt no man designed,
And no man claimed the conquest of your land.
But gropers both through fields of thought confined
We stumble and we do not understand.
You only saw your future bigly planned,
And we, the tapering paths of our own mind.
And in each other's dearest ways we stand,
And hiss and hate. And the blind fight the blind.

When it is peace, then we may view again
With new-won eyes each other's truer form
And wonder. Grown more loving-kind and warm
We'll grasp firm hands and laugh at the old pain,
When it is peace. But until peace, the storm
The darkness and the thunder and the rain.

"ALL THE HILLS AND VALES ALONG"

All the hills and vales along
Earth is bursting into song,
And the singers are the chaps
Who are going to die perhaps.
O sing, marching men.
Till the valleys ring again.
Give your gladness to earth's keeping.
So be glad, when you are sleeping.

Cast away regret and rue,
Think what you are marching to.
Little live, great pass.
Jesus Christ and Barabbas
Were found the same day.
This died, that went his way.
So sing with joyful breath.
For why, you are going to death.
Teeming earth will surely store
All the gladness that you pour.

Earth that never doubts nor fears,
Earth that knows of death, not tears,
Earth that bore with joyful ease
Hemlock for Socrates,

Earth that blossomed and was glad
'Neath the cross that Christ had,
Shall rejoice and blossom too
When the bullet reaches you.
Wherefore, men marching
On the road to death, sing!
Pour your gladness on earth's head.
So be merry, so be dead.

From the hills and valleys earth
Shouts back the sound of mirth.
Tramp of feet and lilt of song
Ringing all the road along.
All the music of their going,
Ringing swinging glad song-throwing,
Earth will echo still, when foot
Lies numb and voice mute.
On, marching men, on
To the gates of death with song.
Sow your gladness for earth's reaping.
So you may be glad, though sleeping.
Strew your gladness on earth's bed.
So be merry, so be dead.

LE REVENANT

He trod the oft-remembered lane
(Now smaller-seeming than before
When first he left his father's door
For newer things), but still quite plain

(Though half-benighted now) upstood
Old landmarks, ghosts across the lane
That brought the Bygone back again:
Shorn haystacks and the rooky wood;

The guide post, too, which once he clomb
To read the figures: fourteen miles
To Swindon, four to Qinton Stiles,
And only half a mile to home:

And far away the one homestead, where—
Behind the day now not quite set
So that he saw in silhouette
Its chimneys still stand black and bare—

He noticed that the trees were not
So big as when he journeyed last
That way. For greatly now he passed

Striding above the hedges, hot

With hopings, as he passed by where
A lamp before him glanced and stayed
Across his path, so that his shade
Seemed like a giant's moving there.

The dullness of the sunken sun
He marked not, nor how dark it grew,
Nor that strange flapping bird that flew
Above: he thought but of the One....

He topped the crest and crossed the fence.
Noticed the garden that it grew
As erst, noticed the hen-house too
(The kennel had been altered since).

It seemed so unchanged and so still.
(Could it but be the past arisen
For one short night from out of prison?)
He reached the big-bowed window-sill.

Lifted the window sash with care,
Then, gaily throwing aside the blind.
Shouted. It was a shock to find
That he was not remembered there.

At once he felt not all his pain,
But murmuringly apologised,
Turned, once more sought the undersized
Blown trees, and the long lanky lane,

Wondering and pondering on, past where
A lamp before him glanced and stayed
Across his path, so that his shade
Seemed like a giant's moving there.

LOST

Across my past imaginings
Has dropped a blindness silent and slow.
My eye is bent on other things
Than those it once did see and know.

I may not think on those dear lands
(O far away and long ago!)
Where the old battered signpost stands
And silently the four roads go

East, west, south and north,
And the cold winter winds do blow.
And what the evening will bring forth
Is not for me nor you to know.

EXPECTANS EXPECTAVI

From morn to midnight, all day through,
I laugh and play as others do,
I sin and chatter, just the same
As others with a different name.

And all year long upon the stage
I dance and tumble and do rage
So vehemently, I scarcely see
The inner and eternal me.

I have a temple I do not
Visit, a heart I have forgot,
A self that I have never met,
A secret shrine—and yet, and yet

This sanctuary of my soul
Unwitting I keep white and whole
Unlatched and lit, if Thou should'st care
To enter or to tarry there.

With parted lips and outstretched hands
And listening ears Thy servant stands,
Call Thou early, call Thou late,
To Thy great service dedicate.

May 1915

TWO SONNETS

I

Saints have adored the lofty soul of you.
Poets have whitened at your high renown.
We stand among the many millions who
Do hourly wait to pass your pathway down.
You, so familiar, once were strange: we tried
To live as of your presence unaware.
But now in every road on every side
We see your straight and steadfast signpost there.

I think it like that signpost in my land
Hoary and tall, which pointed me to go
Upward, into the hills, on the right hand,
Where the mists swim and the winds shriek and blow,
A homeless land and friendless, but a land
I did not know and that I wished to know.

II

Such, such is Death: no triumph: no defeat:
Only an empty pail, a slate rubbed clean,
A merciful putting away of what has been.

And this we know: Death is not Life effete,
Life crushed, the broken pail. We who have seen
So marvellous things know well the end not yet.

Victor and vanquished are a-one in death:
Coward and brave: friend, foe. Ghosts do not say
"Come, what was your record when you drew breath?
But a big blot has hid each yesterday
So poor, so manifestly incomplete.
And your bright Promise, withered long and sped,
Is touched, stirs, rises, opens and grows sweet
And blossoms and is you, when you are dead.

12th June 1915

"WHEN YOU SEE MILLIONS OF THE MOUTHLESS DEAD"

When you see millions of the mouthless dead
Across your dreams in pale battalions go,
Say not soft things as other men have said.
That you'll remember. For you need not so.
Give them not praise. For, deaf, how should they know
It is not curses heaped on each gashed head?
Nor tears. Their blind eyes see not your tears flow.
Nor honour. It is easy to be dead.
Say only this, "They are dead." Then add thereto,
"Yet many a better one has died before."
Then, scanning all the o'ercrowded mass, should you
Perceive one face that you loved heretofore.
It is a spook. None wears the face you knew.
Great death has made all his for evermore.

"THERE IS SUCH CHANGE IN ALL THOSE FIELDS"

There is such change in all those fields,
Such motion rhythmic, ordered, free,
Where ever-glancing summer yields
Birth, fragrance, sunlight, immanency.
To make us view our rights of birth.
What shall we do? How shall we die?
We, captives of a roaming earth.
Mid shades that life and light deny.
Blank summer's surfeit heaves in mist;
Dumb earth basks dewy-washed; while still
We whom Intelligence has kissed
Do make us shackles of our will.
And yet I know in each loud brain,
Round-clamped with laws and learning so,
Is madness more and lust of strain
Than earth's jerked godlings e'er can know.

The false Delilah of our brain
Has set us round the millstone going.
O lust of roving'! lust of pain!
Our hair will not be long in growing.
Like Winded Samson round we go.
We hear the grindstone groan and cry.
Yet we are kings, we know, we know.
What shall we do? How shall we die?

Take but our pauper's gift of birth,
O let us from the grindstone free!
And tread the maddening gladdening earth
In strength close-braced with purity.
The earth is old; we ever new.
Our eyes should see no other sense
Than this, eternally to do—
Our joy, our task, our recompense;
Up unexplored mountains move,
Track tireless through great wastes afar.
Nor slumber in the arms of love.
Nor tremble on the brink of war;
Make Beauty and make Rest give place,
Mock Prudence loud—and she is gone,
Smite Satisfaction on the face
And tread the ghost of Ease upon.
Light-lipped and singing press we hard
Over old earth which now is worn,
Triumphant, buffetted and scarred,
By billows howled at, tempest-torn.
Toward blue horizons far away
(Which do not give the rest we need.
But some long strife, more than this play,
Some task that will be stern indeed)—

We ever new, we ever young.
We happy creatures of a day!
What will the gods say, seeing us strung
As nobly and as taut as they?

"I HAVE NOT BROUGHT MY ODYSSEY"

I have not brought my Odyssey
With me here across the sea;
But you'll remember, when I say
How, when they went down Sparta way.
To sandy Sparta, long ere dawn
Horses were harnessed, rations drawn.
Equipment polished sparkling bright,
And breakfasts swallowed (as the white
Of Eastern heavens turned to gold)—
The dogs barked, swift farewells were told.
The sun springs up, the horses neigh.
Crackles the whip thrice—then away!
From sun-go-up to sun-go-down
All day across the sandy down
The gallant horses galloped, till
The wind across the downs more chill
Blew, the sun sank and all the road
Was darkened, that it only showed
Right at the end the town's red light
And twilight glimmering into night.

The horses never slackened till
They reached the doorway and stood still.
Then came the knock, the unlading; then
The honey-sweet converse of men,
The splendid bath, the change of dress,
Then—O the grandeur of their Mess,
The henchmen, the prim stewardess!
And O the breaking of old ground.
The tales, after the port went round!
(The wondrous wiles of old Odysseus,
Old Agamemnon and his misuse
Of his command, and that young chit
Paris — who didn't care a bit
For Helen — only to annoy her
He did it really, K.T.A.)

But soon they led amidst the din
The honey-sweet ἀοιδός in,
Whose eyes were Wind, whose soul had sight.
Who knew the fame of men in fight—
Bard of white hair and trembling foot,

Who sang whatever God might put
Into his heart.
And there he sung,
Those war-worn veterans among.
Tales of great war and strong hearts wrung,
Of clash of arms, of council's brawl.
Of beauty that must early fall,
Of battle hate and battle joy
By the old windy walls of Troy.
They felt that they were unreal then,
Visions and shadow-forms, not men.
But those the Bard did sing and say
(Some were their comrades, some were they)
Took shape and loomed and strengthened more
Greatly than they had guessed of yore.

And now the fight begins again.
The old war-joy, the old war-pain.
Sons of one school across the sea
We have no fear to fight—

And soon, O soon, I do not doubt it.
With the body or without it.
We shall all come tumbling down
To our old wrinkled red-capped town.
Perhaps the road up Ilsley way.
The old ridge-track, will be my way.
High up among the sheep and sky.
Look down on Wantage, passing by.
And see the smoke from Swindon town;
And then full left at Liddington,
Where the four winds of heaven meet
The earth-blest traveller to greet.
And then my face is toward the south.
There is a singing on my mouth:

Away to rightward I descry
My Barbury ensconced in sky,
Far underneath the Osbourne twins,
And at my feet the thyme and whins.
The grasses with their little crowns
Of gold, the lovely Aldbourne downs,
And that old signpost (well I knew
That crazy signpost, arms askew,
Old mother of the four grass ways).
And then my mouth is dumb with praise,
For, past the wood and chalkpit tiny,
A glimpse of Marlborough ἐρατεινή!
So I descend beneath the rail
To warmth and welcome and wassail.

This from the battered trenches—rough.
Jingling and tedious enough.
And so I sign myself to you:
One, who some crooked pathways knew

Round Bedwyn: who could scarcely leave
The Downs on a December eve:
Was at his happiest in shorts,
And got—not many good reports!
Small skill of rhyming in his hand—
But you'll forgive—you'll understand.

12th July 1915

IN MEMORIAM

There is no fitter end than this.
No need is now to yearn nor sigh.
We know the glory that is his,
A glory that can never die.

Surely we knew it long before,
Knew all along that he was made
For a swift radiant morning, for
A sacrificing swift night-shade.

8th September 1915

BEHIND THE LINES

We are now at the end of a few days' rest, a kilometre behind the lines. Except for the farmyard noises (new style) it might almost be the little village that first took us to its arms six weeks ago. It has been a fine day, following on a day's rain, so that the earth smells like spring. I have just managed to break off a long conversation with the farmer in charge, a tall thin stooping man with sad eyes, in trouble about his land: les Anglais stole his peas, trod down his corn and robbed his young potatoes: he told it as a father telling of infanticide. There may have been fifteen francs' worth of damage done; he will never get compensation out of those shifty Belgian burgomasters; but it was not exactly the fifteen francs but the invasion of the soil that had been his for forty years, in which the weather was his only enemy, that gave him a kind of Niobe's dignity to his complaint.

Meanwhile there is the usual evening sluggishness. Close by, a quick firer is pounding away its allowance of a dozen shells a day. It is like a cow coughing. Eastward there begins a sound (all sounds begin at sundown and continue intermittently till midnight, reaching their zenith at about 9 p.m. and then dying away as sleepiness claims their masters)—a sound like a motor-cycle race— thousands of motor-cycles tearing round and round a track, with cut-outs out: it is really a pair of machine guns firing. And now one sound awakens another. The old cow coughing has started the motor-bykes: and now at intervals of a few minutes come express trains in our direction: you can hear them rushing toward us; they pass going straight for the town behind us: and you hear them begin to slow down as they reach the town: they will soon stop: but no, every time, just before they reach it, is a tremendous railway accident. At least, it must be a railway accident, there is so much noise, and you can see the dust that the wreckage scatters. Sometimes the train behind comes very close, but it too smashes on the wreckage of its forerunners. A tremendous cloud of dust, and then the groans. So many trains and accidents start the cow coughing again: only another cow this time, somewhere behind us, a tremendous sized cow, *θαυμάσιον ὅσον*, with awful whooping-cough. It must be a buffalo: this cough must burst its sides. And now someone starts sliding down the stairs on a tin tray, to soften the heart of the cow, make it laugh and cure its cough. The din he makes is appalling. He is beating the tray with a broom now, every two minutes a stroke: he has certainly stopped the cow by this time, probably killed it. He will leave off soon (thanks to the "shell tragedy"): we know he can't last.

It is now almost dark: come out and see the fireworks. While waiting for them to begin you can notice how pale and white the corn is in the summer twilight: no wonder with all this whooping cough about. And the motor-cycles: notice how all these races have at least a hundred entries: there is never a single cycle going. And why are there no birds coming back to roost? Where is the lark? I haven't heard him all to-day. He must have got whooping-cough as well, or be staying at home through fear of the cow. I think it will rain to-morrow, but there have been no swallows circling low, stroking their breasts on the full ears of corn. Anyhow, it is night now, but the circus does not close till twelve. Look! there is the first of them! The fireworks are beginning. Red flares shooting up high into the night, or skimming low over the ground, like the swallows that are not: and rockets bursting into stars. See how they illumine that patch of ground a mile in front. See it, it is deadly pale in their searching light: ghastly, I think, and featureless except for two big lines of eyebrows ashy white, parallel along it, raised a little from its surface. Eyebrows. Where are the eyes? Hush, there are no eyes. What those shooting flares illumine is a mole. A long thin mole. Burrowing by day and shoving a timorous enquiring snout above the ground by night. Look, did you see it? No, you cannot see it from here. But were you a good deal nearer, you would see behind that snout a long and endless row of sharp shining teeth. The rockets catch the light from these teeth and the teeth glitter: they are silently removed from the poison-spitting gums of the mole. For the mole's gums spit fire and, they say, send something more concrete than fire darting into the night. Even when its teeth are off. But you cannot see all this from here: you can only see the rockets and then for a moment the pale ground beneath. But it is quite dark now.

And now for the fun of the fair! You will hear soon the riding-master crack his whip—why, there it is. Listen, a thousand whips are cracking, whipping the horses round the ring. At last! The fun of the circus is begun. For the motor-cycle team race has started off again: and the whips are cracking all: and the waresman starts again, beating his loud tin tray to attract the customers: and the cows in the cattle-show start coughing, coughing: and the firework display is at its best: and the circus specials come one after another bearing the merry makers back to town, all to the inevitable crash, the inevitable accident. It can't last long: these accidents are so frequent, they'll all get soon killed off, I hope. Yes, it is diminishing. The train service is cancelled (and time too): the cows have stopped coughing: and the cycle race is done. Only the kids who have bought new whips at the fair continue to crack them: and unused rockets that lie about the ground are still sent up occasionally. But now the children are being driven off to bed: only an occasional whip-crack now (perhaps the child is now the sufferer): and the tired showmen going over the ground pick up the rocket-sticks and dead flares. At least I suppose this is what must be happening: for occasionally they still find one that has not gone off and send it up out of mere perversity. Else what silence!

It must be midnight now. Yes, it is midnight. But before you go to bed, bend down, put your ear against the ground. What do you hear? "I hear an endless tapping and a tramping to and fro: both

are muffled: but they come from everywhere. Tap, tap, tap: pick, pick, pick: tra-mp, tra-mp, tra-mp."
So you see the circus-goers are not all gone to sleep. There is noise coming from the womb of earth,
noise of men who tap and mine and dig and pass to and fro on their watch. What you have seen is
the foam and froth of war: but underground is labour and throbbing and long watch. Which will one
day bear their fruit. They will set the circus on fire. Then what pandemonium! Let us hope it will not
be to-morrow!

15th July 1915

A CALL TO ACTION

I

A thousand years have passed away,
Cast back your glances on the scene.
Compare this England of to-day
With England as she once has been.

Fast beat the pulse of living then:
The hum of movement, throb of war.
The rushing mighty sound of men
Reverberated loud and far.

They girt their loins up and they trod
The path of danger, rough and high;
For Action, Action was their god,
"Be up and doing" was their cry.

A thousand years have passed away;
The sands of life are running low;
The world is sleeping out her day;
The day is dying—be it so.

A thousand years have passed amain;
The sands of life are running thin;
Thought is our leader—Thought is vain;
Speech is our goddess—Speech is sin.

II

It needs no thought to understand,
No speech to tell, nor sight to see
That there has come upon our land
The curse of Inactivity.

We do not see the vital point

That 'tis the eighth, most deadly, sin
To wail, "The world is out of joint"—
And not attempt to put it in.

We see the swollen stream of crime
Flow hourly past us, thick and wide;
We gaze with interest for a time,
And pass by on the other side.

We see the tide of human sin
Rush roaring past our very door.
And scarcely one man plunges in
To drag the drowning to the shore.

We, dull and dreamy, stand and blink.
Forgetting glory, strength and pride.
Half-listless watchers on the brink.
Half-ruined victims of the tide.

III

We question, answer, make defence.
We sneer, we scoff, we criticize.
We wail and moan our decadence,
Enquire, investigate, surmise;

We preach and prattle, peer and pry
And fit together two and two:
We ponder, argue, shout, swear, lie—
We will not, for we cannot, do.

Pale puny soldiers of the pen.
Absorbed in this your inky strife.
Act as of old, when men were men
England herself and life yet life.

October 1912

RAIN

When the rain is coming down,
And all Court is still and bare.
And the leaves fall wrinkled, brown,
Through the kindly winter air.
And in tattered flannels I
'Sweat' beneath a tearful sky,
And the sky is dim and grey.
And the rain is coming down,

And I wander far away
From the little red-capped town:
There is something in the rain
That would bid me to remain:
There is something in the wind
That would whisper, "Leave behind
All this land of time and rules.
Land of bells and early schools.

Latin, Greek and College food
Do you precious little good.
Leave them: if you would be free
Follow, follow, after me!"

When I reach 'Four Miler's' height,
And I look abroad again
On the skies of dirty white
And the drifting veil of rain,
And the bunch of scattered hedge
Dimly swaying on the edge.
And the endless stretch of downs
Clad in green and silver gowns;
There is something in their dress
Of bleak barren ugliness,
That would whisper, "You have read
Of a land of light and glory:
But believe not what is said.
'Tis a kingdom bleak and hoary,
Where the winds and tempests call
And the rain sweeps over all.

Heed not what the preachers say
Of a good land far away.
Here's a better land and kind
And it is not far to find."

Therefore, when we rise and sing
Of a distant land, so fine.
Where the bells for ever ring,
And the suns for ever shine:
Singing loud and singing grand.
Of a happy far-off land,
O! I smile to hear the song.
For I know that they are wrong.
That the happy land and gay
Is not very far away,
And that I can get there soon
Any rainy afternoon.

And when summer comes again,
And the downs are dimpling green.

And the air is free from rain,
And the clouds no longer seen:
Then I know that they have gone
To find a new camp further on.
Where there is no shining sun
To throw light on what is done,
Where the summer can't intrude
On the fort where winter stood:
      —Only blown and drenching grasses,
      Only rain that never passes.
      Moving mists and sweeping wind,
      And I follow them behind!

October 1915

A TALE OF TWO CAREERS

I

SUCCESS

He does not dress as other men,
His 'kish' is loud and gay,
His 'side' is as the 'side' of ten
Because his 'barnes' are grey.

His head has swollen to a size
Beyond the proper size for heads.
He metaphorically buys
The ground on which he treads.

Before his face of haughty grace
The ordinary mortal cowers:
A 'forty-cap' has put the chap
Into another world from ours.

The funny little world that lies
Twixt High Street and the Mound
Is just a swarm of buzzing flies
That aimlessly go round:

If one is stronger in the limb
Or better able to work hard,
It's quite amusing to watch him
Ascending heavenward.

But if one cannot work or play
(Who loves the better part too well).
It's really sad to see the lad

Retained compulsorily in hell.

II

FAILURE

We are the wasters, who have no
Hope in this world here, neither fame,
Because we cannot collar low
Nor write a strange dead tongue the same
As strange dead men did long ago.

We are the weary, who begin
The race with joy, but early fail,
Because we do not care to win
A race that goes not to the frail
And humble: only the proud come in.

We are the shadow-forms, who pass
Unheeded hence from work and play.
We are to-day, but like the grass
That to-day is, we pass away;
And no one stops to say 'Alas!'

Though we have little, all we have
We give our School. And no return
We can expect for what we gave;
No joys; only a summons stern,
"Depart, for others entrance crave!"

As soon as she can clearly prove
That from us is no hope of gain.
Because we only bring her love
And cannot bring her strength or brain,
She tells us, "Go: it is enough."

She turns us out at seventeen,
We may not know her any more,
And all our life with her has been
A life of seeing others score.
While we sink lower and are mean.

We have seen others reap success
Full-measure. None has come to us.
Our life has been one failure. Yes,
But does not God prefer it thus?
God does not also praise success.

And for each failure that we meet,
And for each place we drop behind,

Each toil that holds our aching feet.
Each star we seek and never find,
God, knowing, gives us comfort meet.

The School we care for has not cared
To cherish nor keep our names to be
Memorials. God hath prepared
Some better thing for us, for we
His hopes have known, His failures shared.

November 1912

PEACE

There is silence in the evening when the long days cease,
And a million men are praying for an ultimate release
From strife and sweat and sorrow—they are praying for peace.
        But God is marching on.

Peace for a people that is striving to be free!
Peace for the children of the wild wet sea!
Peace for the seekers of the promised land—do we
        Want peace when God has none?

We pray for rest and beauty that we know we cannot earn,
And ever are we asking for a honey-sweet return;
But God will make it bitter, make it bitter, till we learn
        That with tears the race is run.

And did not Jesus perish to bring to men, not peace,
But a sword, a sword for battle and a sword that should not cease?

Two thousand years have passed us. Do we still want peace
        Where the sword of Christ has shone?

Yes, Christ perished to present us with a sword.
That strife should be our portion and more strife our reward.
For toil and tribulation and the glory of the Lord
        And the sword of Christ are one.

If you want to know the beauty of the thing called rest.
Go, get it from the poets, who will tell you it is best
(And their words are sweet as honey) to lie flat upon your chest
        And sleep till life is gone.

I know that there is beauty where the low streams run.
And the weeping of the willows and the big sunk sun.
But I know my work is doing and it never shall be done.
        Though I march for ages on.

Wild is the tumult of the long grey street,
O, is it never silent from the tramping of their feet?
Here, Jesus, is Thy triumph, and here the world's defeat.
      For from here all peace has gone.

There's a stranger thing than beauty in the ceaseless city's breast,
In the throbbing of its fever—and the wind is in the west.
And the rain is driving forward where there is no rest.
      For the Lord is marching on.

December 1912

THE RIVER

He watched the river running black
Beneath the blacker sky;
It did not pause upon its track
Of silent instancy.
It did not hasten, nor was slack.
But still went gliding by.

It was so black. There was no wind
Its patience to defy.
It was not that the man had sinned.
Or that he wished to die.
Only the wide and silent tide
Went slowly sweeping by.

The mass of blackness moving down
Filled full of dreams the eye;
The lights of all the lighted town
Upon its breast did lie.
The tall black trees were upside down
In the river's phantasy.

He had an envy for its black
Inscrutability;
He felt impatiently the lack
Of that great law whereby
The river never travels back
But still goes gliding by;

But still goes gliding by, nor clings
To passing things that die,
Nor shows the secrets that it brings
From its strange source on high.
And he felt "We are two living things
And the weaker one is I."

He saw the town, that having stack
Piled up against the sky.
He saw the river running black
On, on and on: O, why—
Could he not move along his track
With such consistency?

He had a yearning for the strength
That comes of unity:
The union of one soul at length
With its twin-soul to lie:
To be a part of one great strength
That moves and cannot die.

He watched the river running black
Beneath the blacker sky.
He pulled his coat about his back.
He did not strive nor cry.
He put his foot upon the track
That still went gliding by

The thing that never travels back
Received him silently.
And there was left no shred, no wrack
To show the reason why:
Only the river running black
Beneath the blacker sky.

February 1913

THE SEEKERS

He gates are open on the road
That leads to beauty and to God.

Perhaps the gates are not so fair,
Nor quite so bright as once they were.
When God Himself on earth did stand
And gave to Abraham His hand
And led him to a better land.

For lo! the unclean walk therein,
And those that have been soiled with sin.
The publican and harlot pass
Along: they do not stain its grass.
In it the needy has his share,
In it the foolish do not err.
Yes, spurned and fool and sinner stray

Along the highway and the way.

And what if all its ways are trod
By those whom sin brings near to God?
This journey soon will make them clean;
Their faith is greater than their sin.
For still they travel slowly by
Beneath the promise of the sky.
Scorned and rejected utterly;
Unhonoured; things of little worth
Upon the highroads of this earth;
Afflicted, destitute and weak:
Nor find the beauty that they seek.
The God they set their trust upon:
—Yet still they march rejoicing on.

March 1913